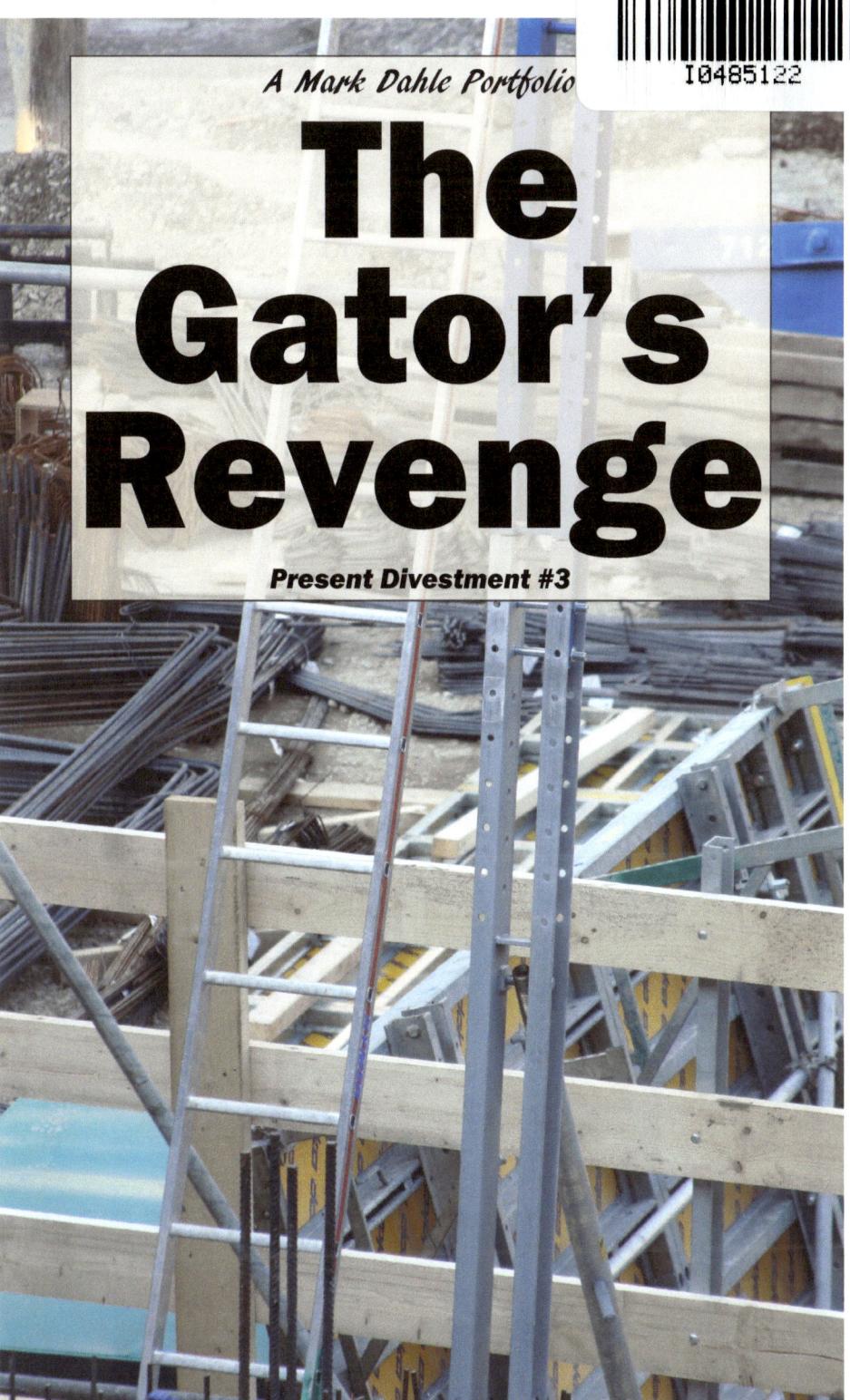

A Mark Dahle Portfolio

The Gator's Revenge

Present Divestment #3

Mark Dahle Portfolios can be read in a few minutes and enjoyed for a lifetime.

This portfolio includes the third story in the Present Divestment series, a photo of a beautiful 36 x 24 inch painting (at the right) and twenty-four outstanding photographs from Basel, Switzerland.

Unlike many picture books, the text is unrelated to the paintings and photographs. This might seem weird at first. One thing that helps is to order more portfolios until you get used to it.

Photographs in this book are available in limited editions. See http://www.MarkDahle.com for more information and for previews of upcoming portfolios.

We do our best to create portfolios free of editing mistakes. But it's hard to catch everything. We reward people who report errors in any Mark Dahle portfolio. For details see MarkDahle.com/Typos.html or send an email to MarkDahle@aol.com with the subject line "Typos." Thanks!

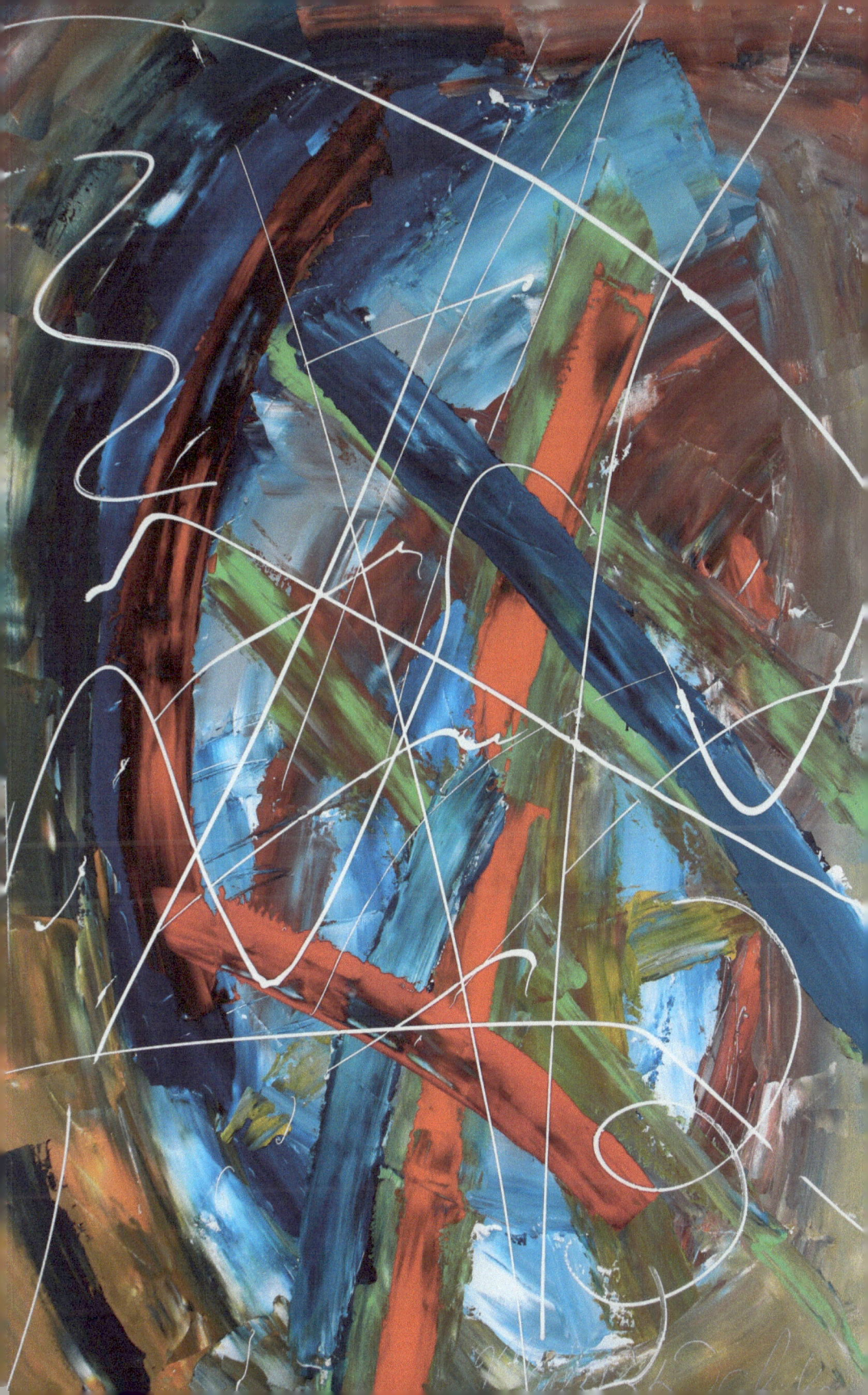

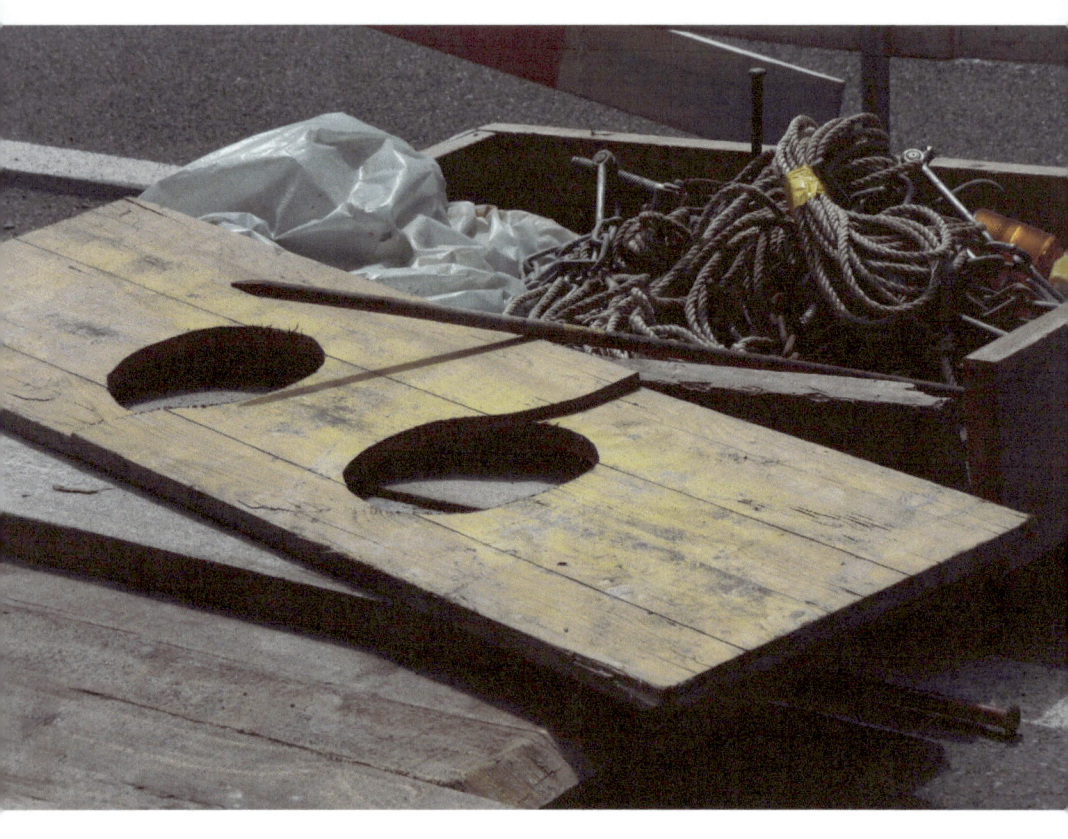

J-rex was frustrated and angry about how Trip 21 had gone. He didn't like loose ends. But it didn't seem like there was anything he could do until the next launch.

He clenched his teeth reflexively. Se wasn't supposed to go this early. The engineers were still a year from stabilizing the process, and J-rex had wanted to use Jon until it was safe. But that wasn't possible now.

J-rex would have to find someone to replace Se. That wasn't going to be easy.

J-rex had kept the Director informed of what little data they had. Now J-rex was showering, taking his first break in five days. And then it came to him. That look in Lat's eyes. He'd seen it before, during training. It meant Lat was onto something, worried about something, but he couldn't pin it down. He was keeping his mouth shut until he figured it out. Lat had the best instincts of anyone J-rex knew. Why had Lat been worried when he had been about to take his first break in five days?

J-rex scrambled to shut off the water. His own break was over. Lat was almost *never* worried. So there must be something J-rex should not have missed.

J-rex knew by experience that when Lat worried, J-rex needed to worry. A lot. J-rex dressed rapidly and raced to his station in the remote control tower.

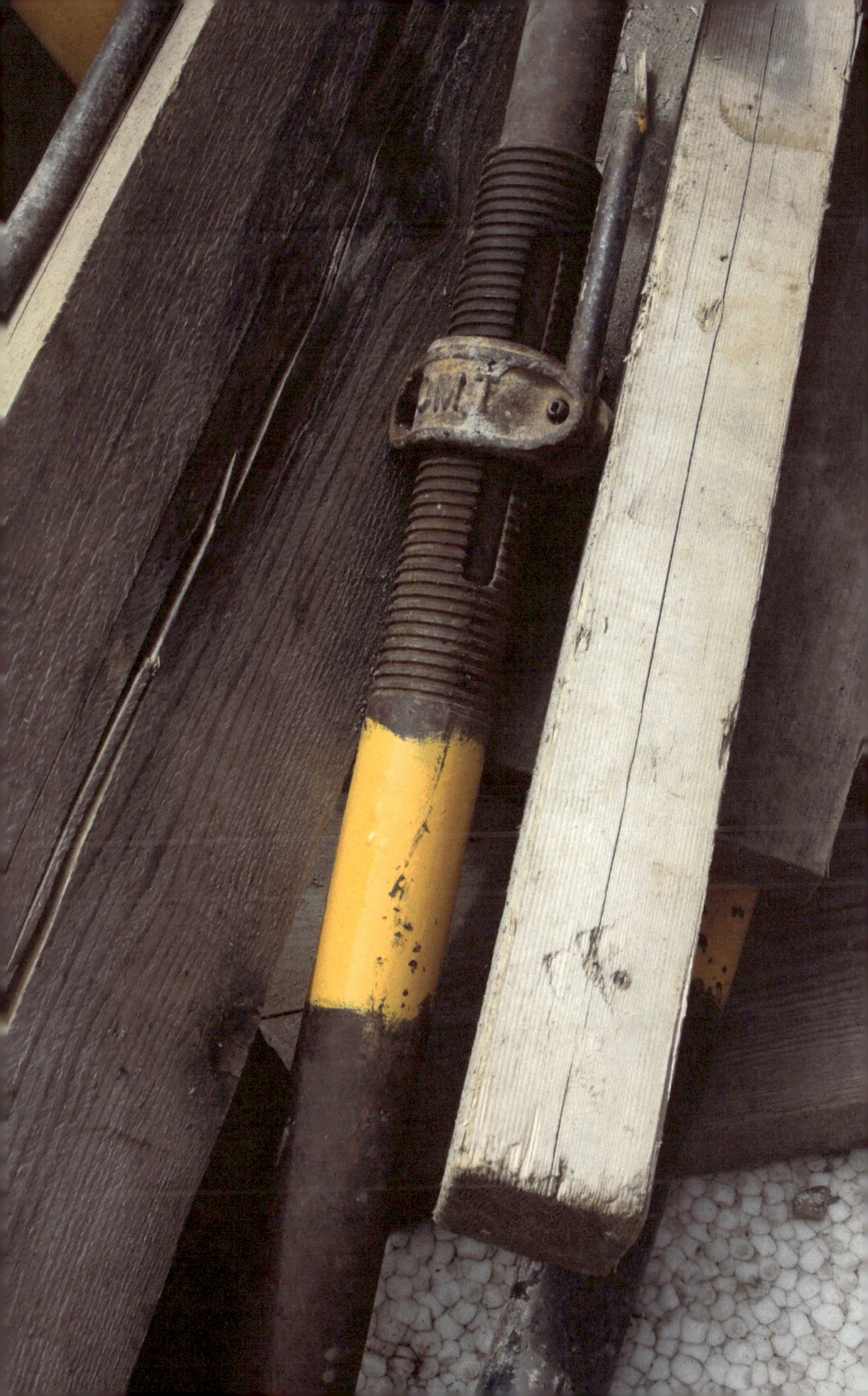

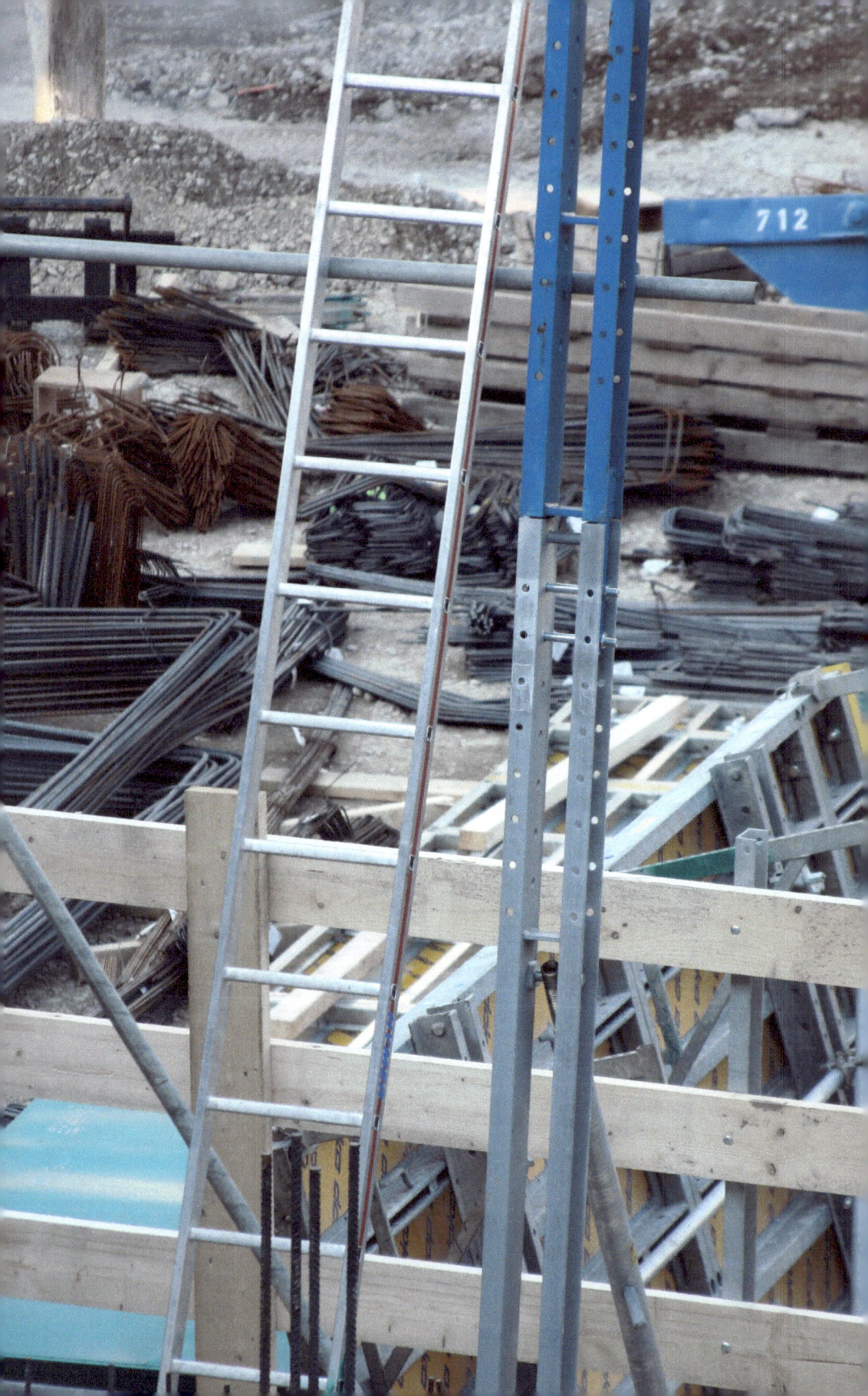

When J-rex ran into the control room, he intended to pour over Lat's data and recheck it, hoping to spot whatever anomaly Lat had noticed. But he didn't need to. When he arrived, half the alarm lights in the tower were blinking red.

J-rex was stunned. He'd only been gone ten minutes. How could so much go wrong in such a short time? Everything had been fine when he had left.

Now every monitor he glanced at showed smashed equipment. He counted three small fires. He could see sparks showering from several locations. Black smoke and thick haze obscured the view of most of the cameras.

J-rex couldn't see the cause of the damage – but he surmised that whoever created the mayhem had taken the gator. The DeepFreeze where the gator had been stored after its autopsy was forced open. The gator wasn't inside.

J-rex sent an InstaText to his team, recalling them immediately and telling them to wait outside the Decontamination Chamber. They were to let the SecurPatrol go in first, weapons ready.

He also texted for two backup SecurPatrols and a lockdown of the area – nobody was allowed out until he gave the order.

And then, finally, he saw a sudden movement in the haze on a monitor on the left.

That's at least *one* of the perpetrators, he thought. He was still guessing the damage was being caused by a team, given how extensive it was.

The figure was hidden in the smoke, so he couldn't see who it was. Then, while he was watching, a massive tail whipped out of the haze and smashed Transporter One – the transporter Se was scheduled to use in three days.

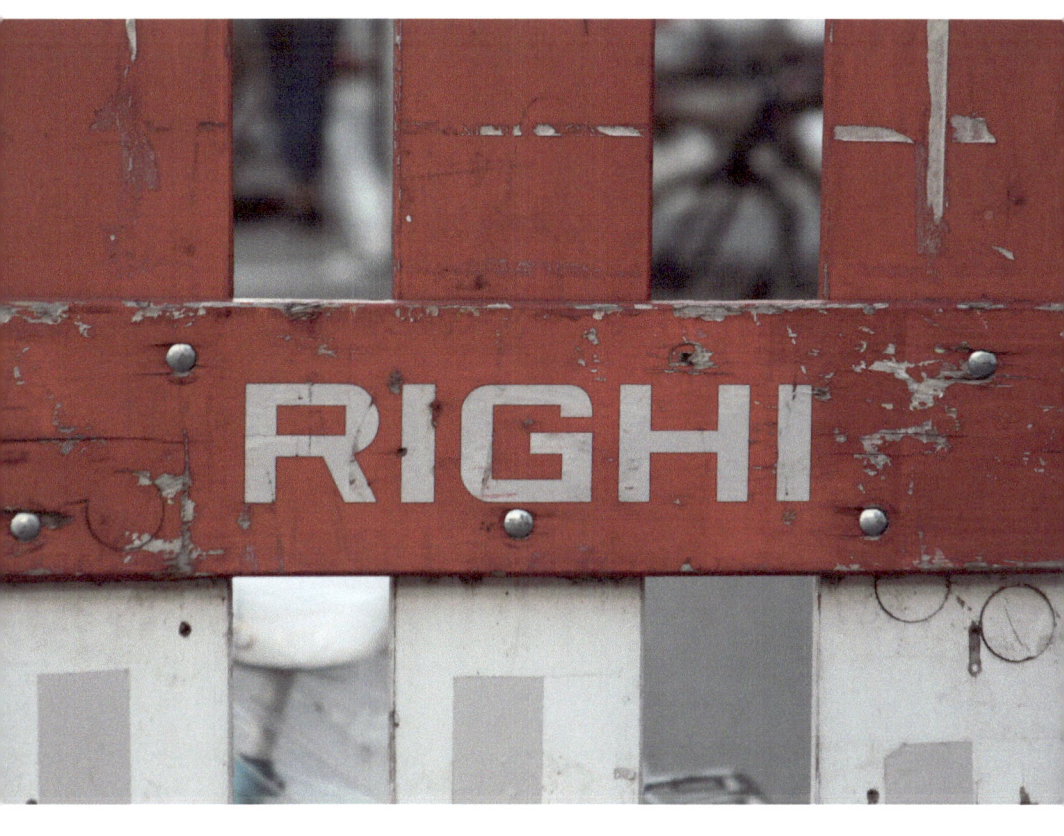

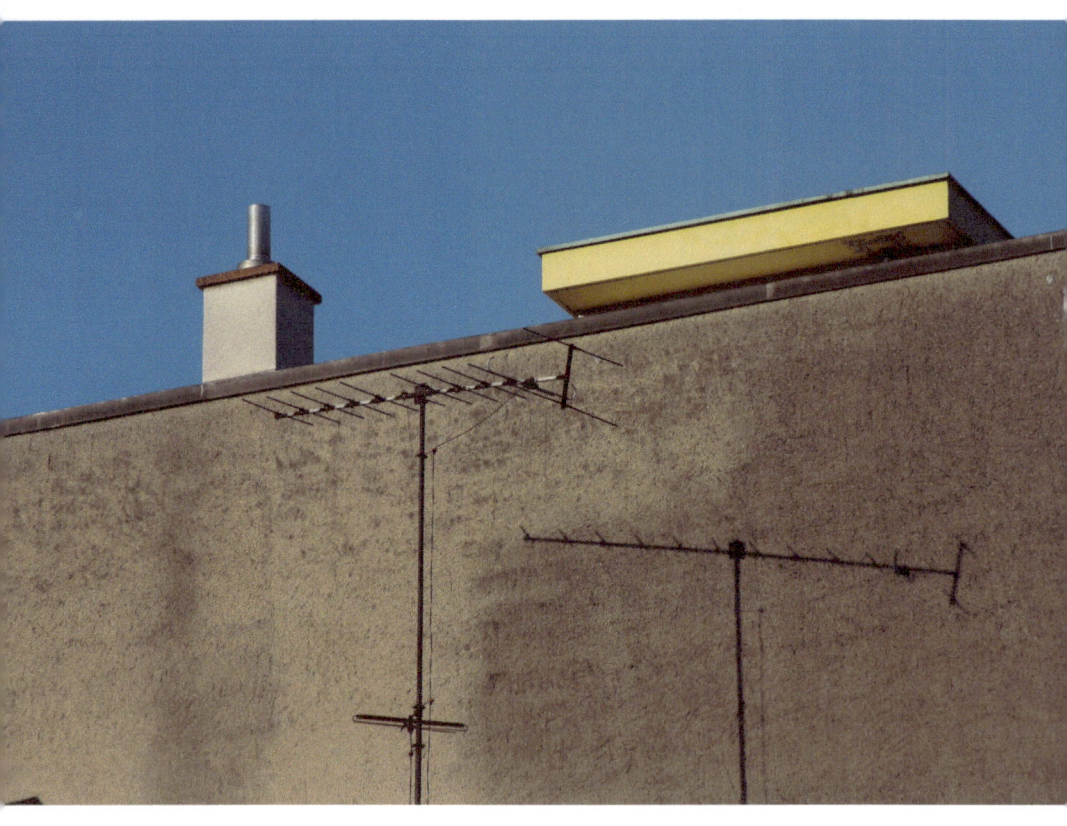

J-rex had had a clear view, but when the tail retreated back into the smoke, he blinked, not quite believing his eyes. Who could hurl the gator with that much force?

J-rex needed his team back *now*.

J-rex could imagine the reactions from his scattered team as they got the recall. Most would assume it was a drill, one more training event in case of future disaster. But the future had arrived. Whatever this was, it was no drill.

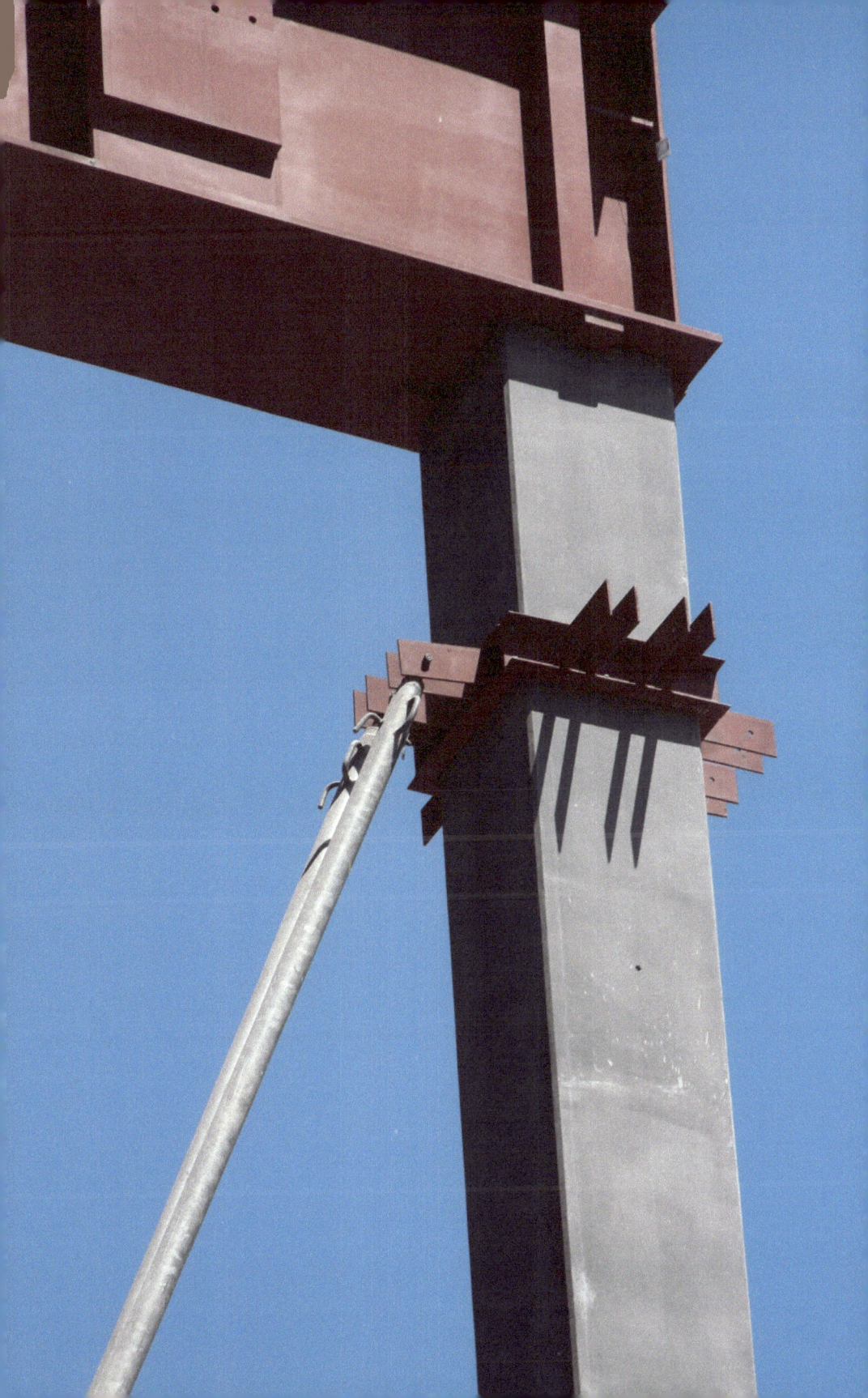

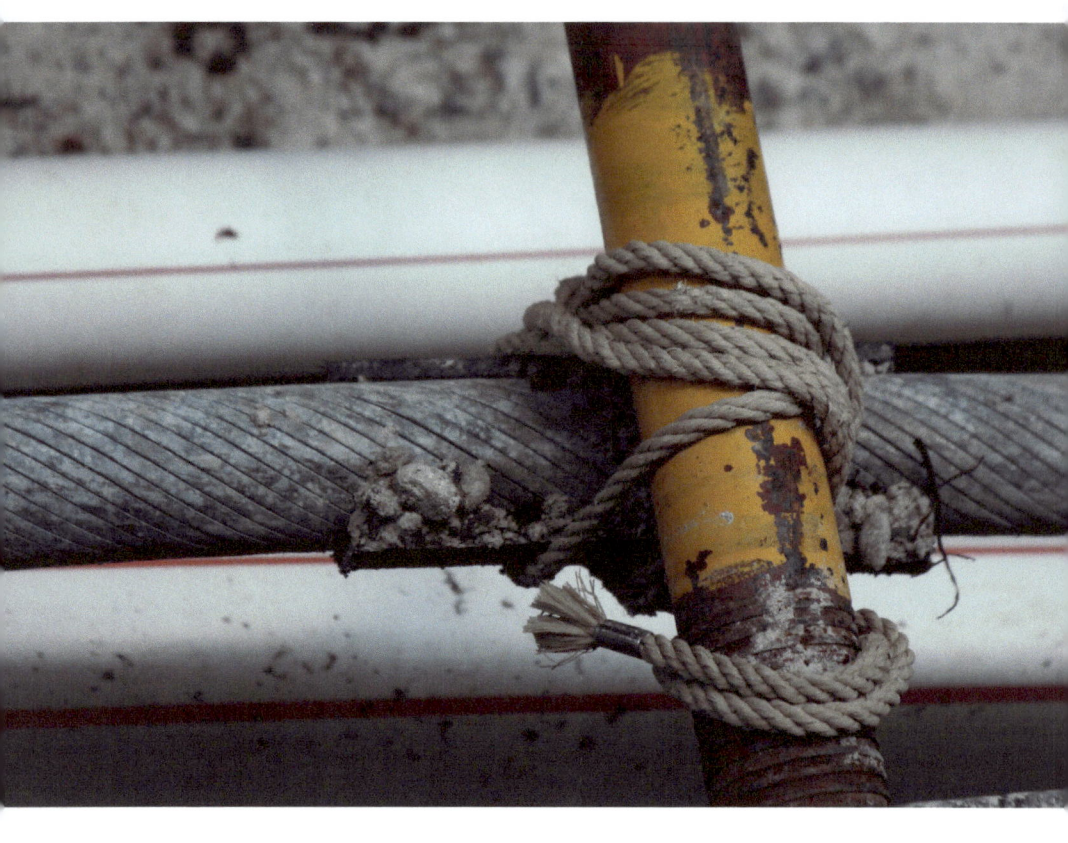

J-rex watched the monitors and alarms and thought about his team. Some of them would already be resting in barracks or (more likely) ClubX. Others would be on the Tube heading to downtown apartments, condos and clubs. Good thing they would be back soon.

Good thing they . . . . He blinked again. Had he really seen that? The smoke had briefly parted in front of a camera and he had seen what looked like a gator moving. On its own. Without anyone around it. . . .

J-rex quickly backed up the video and zoomed in. There was a clear shot, briefly. The gator stepped into the view of a camera and out of it. There was no one around it.

J-rex replayed the video again. He could see the sutures from the autopsy. He could see the bad leg. It was the gator that had been diagnosed as dead for three days. He was still watching the replay when, on the live screen for that same camera, he saw a flick of the gator's tail and the live screen went black.

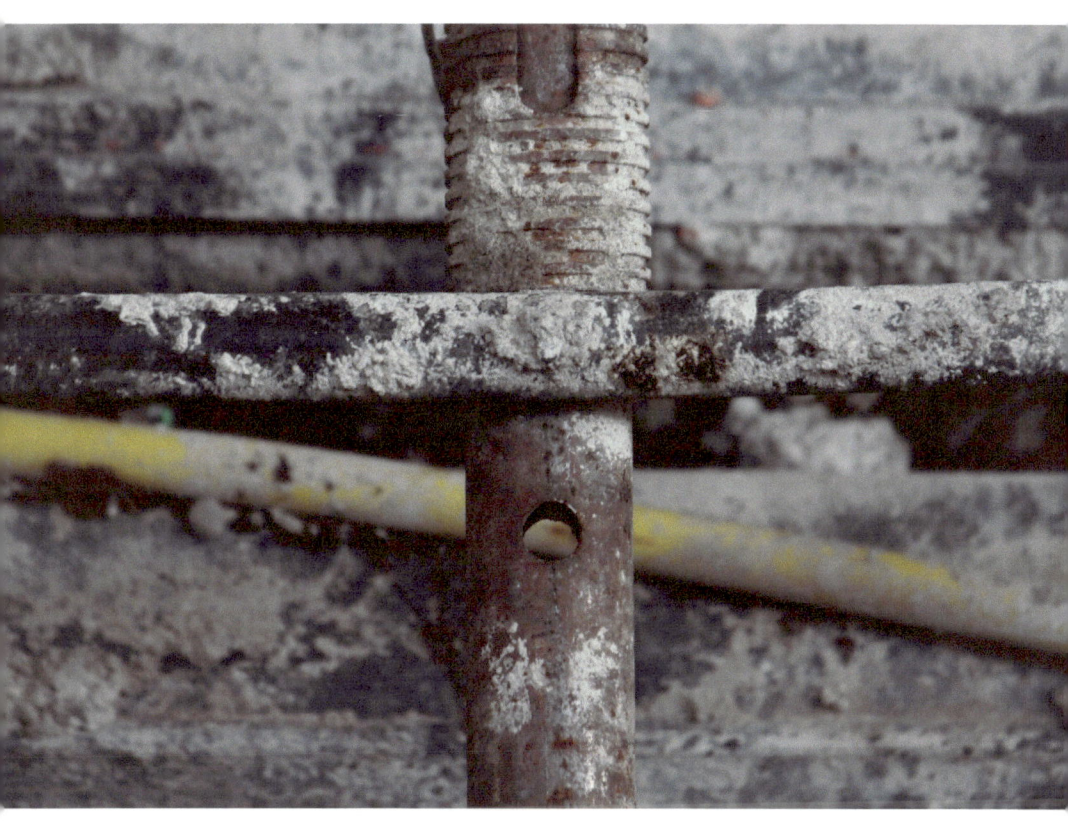

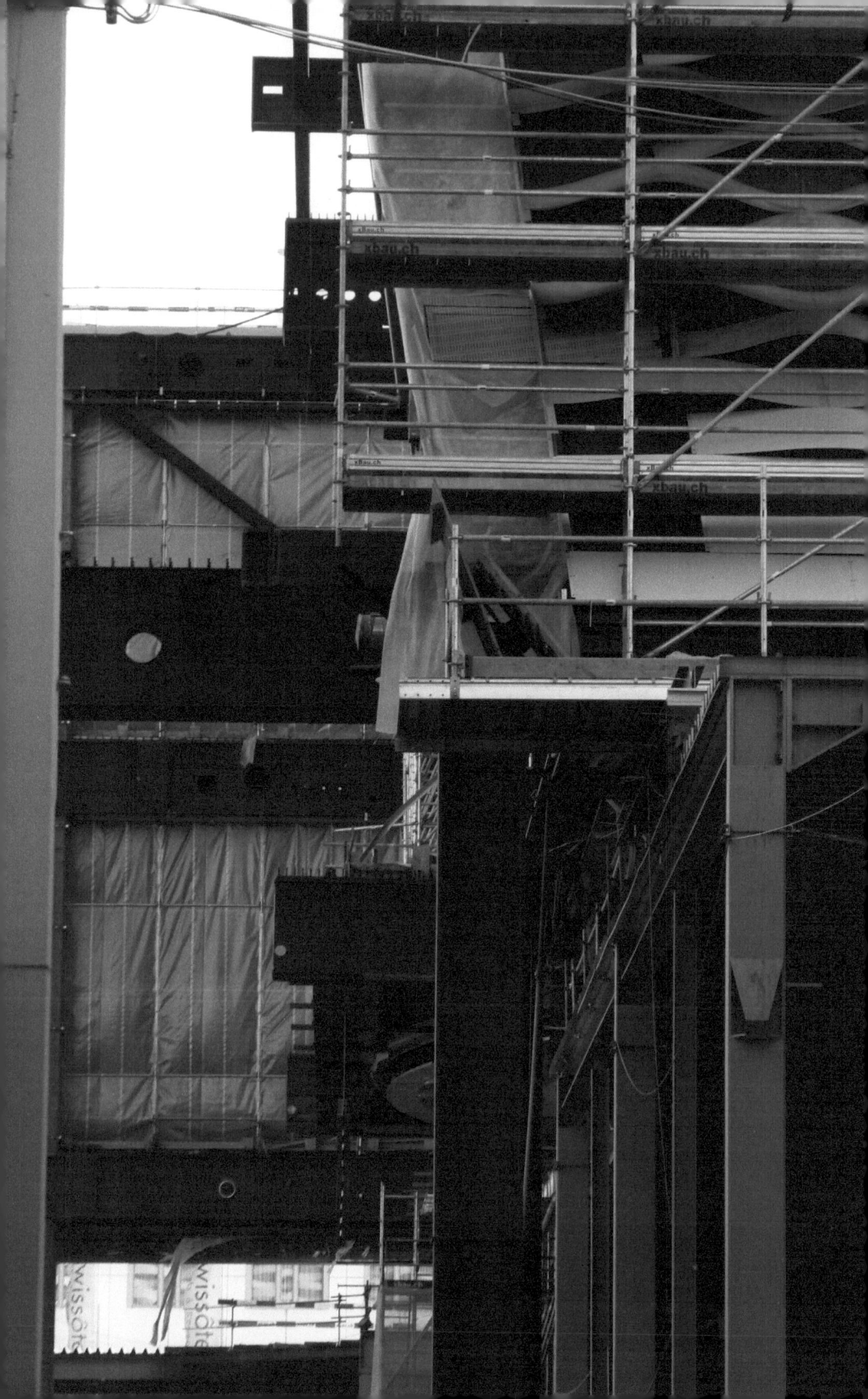

J-rex reviewed the video twice more to be sure. Then he called the Director.

"Sir," he said, "we have a serious problem. Plant Nine needs to go to level ten."

"TEN? A half hour ago you told me four."

"You know the gator we autopsied and examined? It isn't dead. A few minutes ago I sent everyone home for a break. Somehow with everyone gone the gator came back to life. I've got no idea how it could have happened – especially since we detected no life for three days. But I've reviewed the video four times. It's the same gator. I can see the marks from the autopsy. It's even smashed Transporter One."

"Transporter One? That's no good. Two isn't ready. How bad is One damaged?"

"I don't know. The gator has taken out about half the cameras. But if we go to level ten now we can contain this before it gets worse."

"We're not going to ten," the Director said. "Lucky for you, there's a separate problem in Plant Six. Because of that, I'll go to level nine. I'll tell a few Senators and the Vice President to take vacations, just in case. It'll be a media uproar when they leave unexpectedly, but they'll be safe. It'll give you some time to work things out. But we're NOT going to level ten. Nine. That's it."

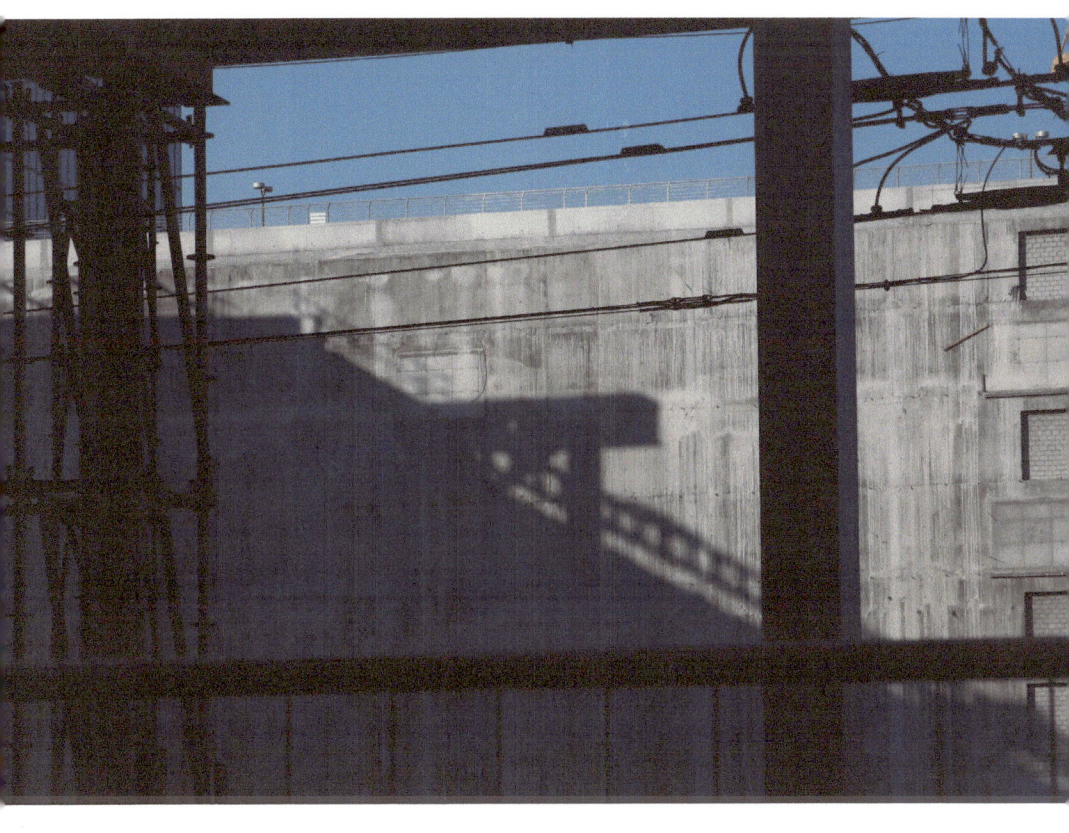

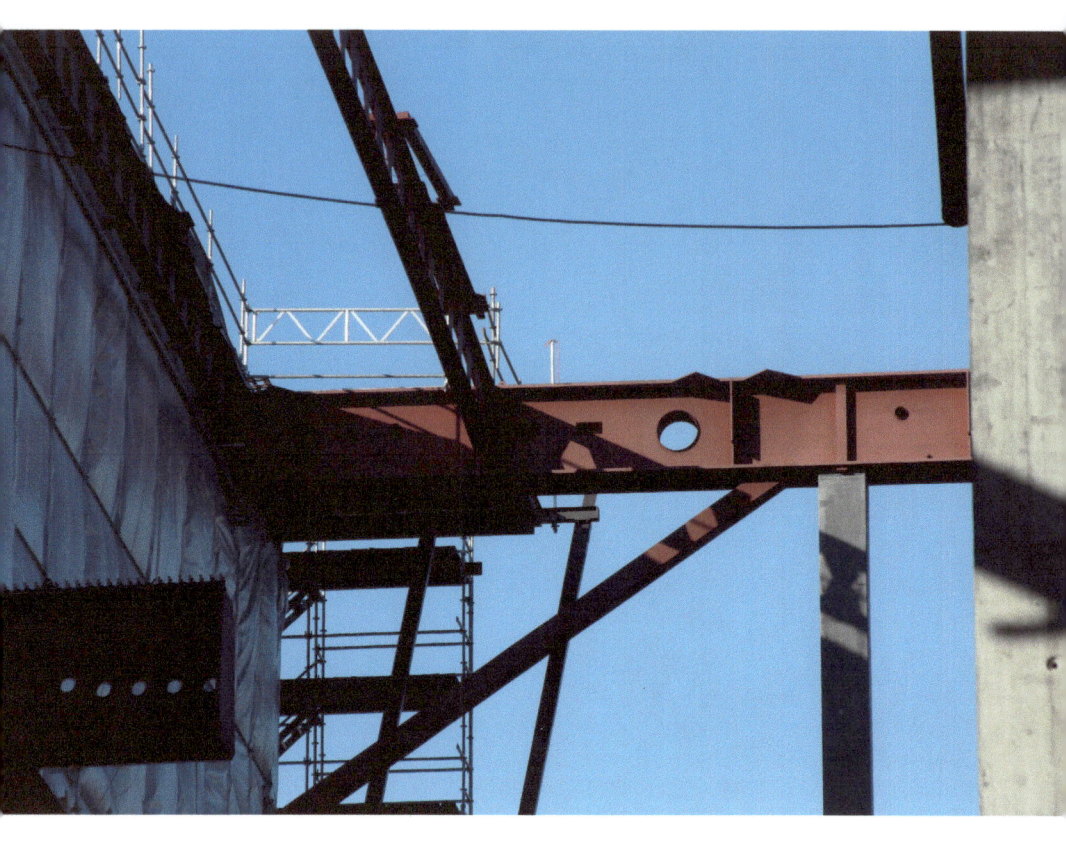

"Sir, level nine doesn't make sense. There's no need to evacuate anyone. If we go to ten, we control the damage. All we lose is the plant itself. We won't lose any research – that's all backed up elsewhere. We won't lose Transporter One – that's already broken. All we lose is a prototype that isn't ready yet."

"I'm not losing Transporter Two and everything else in the plant just because you can't figure out how to handle a common aligator."

"Sir . . . ." But the line was dead. The Director had hung up.

J-rex realized he should have used hyptrolysis on the Director, but it was too late.

Nine. That, J-rex thought, could be worse than leaving things at level four. If enough people noticed the evacuations, it could cause a panic. And it made no sense strategically unless Plant Six was *really* in a mess.

Fortunately, he thought, in another five or ten minutes he would have his team back. In the meantime, he had one more call to make.

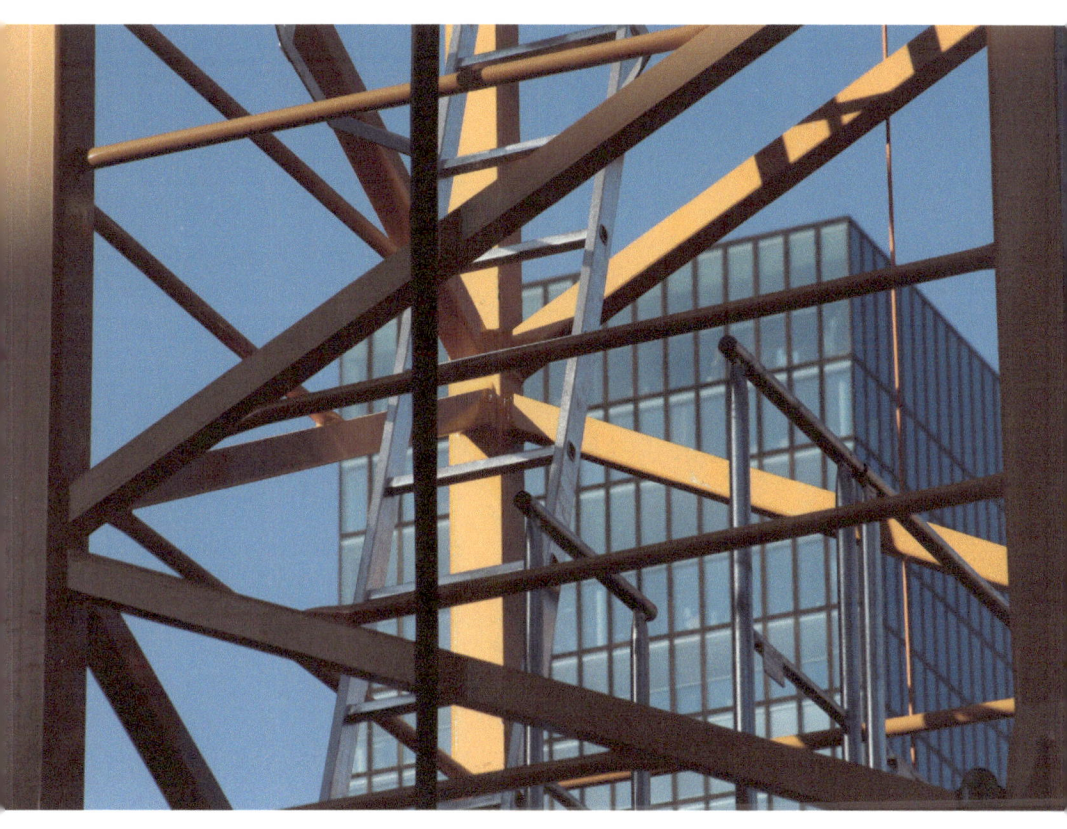

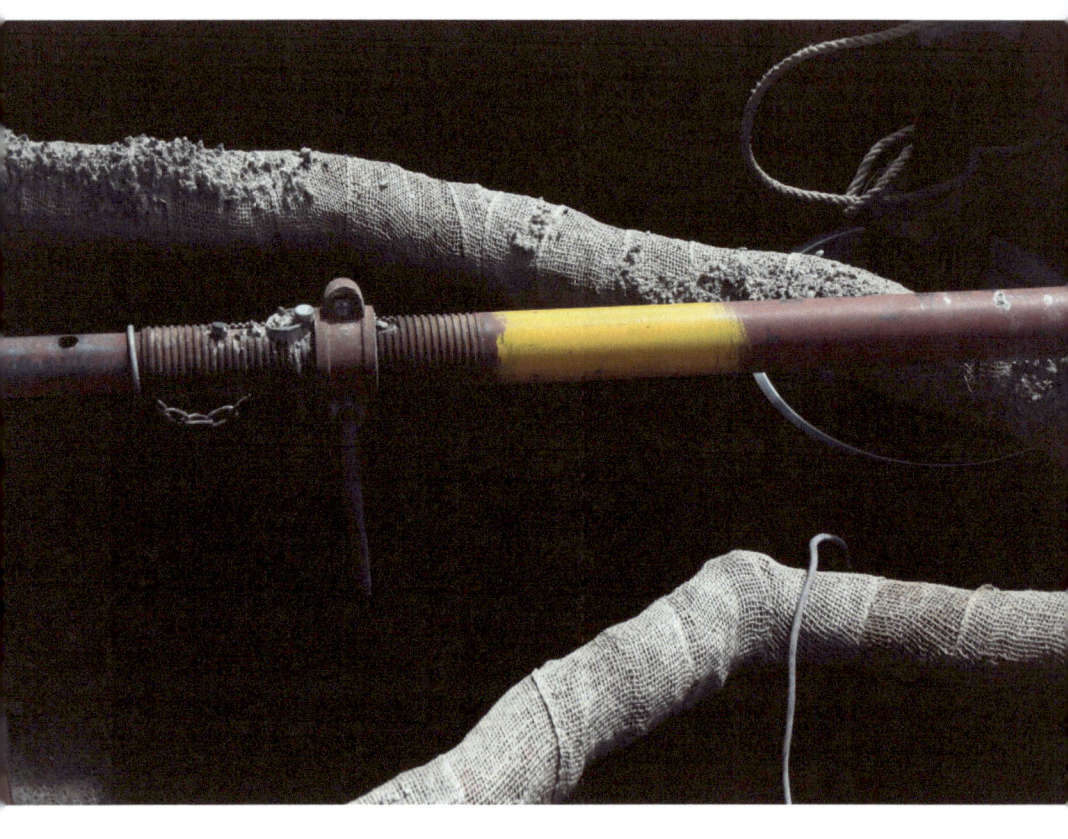

J-rex was safe in the Remote. In the Remote, it didn't matter how high the count went. And his team would be safe once they got back to the launch site, unless the count went to ten. Or unless the mayhem got worse. But his family. . . .

J-rex called Lisa.

"Hi!" Lisa said. "You've been out of contact so long! I'm at the MallUniverse. Want to join me for lunch?"

"I'd love to, babe. But listen carefully." That was the phrase he used to put her under hyptrolysis. He wouldn't repeat his mistake of not using it with the Director. "I just talked to the Director. Our plant should be at level ten."

"Ten?" Tears started to form in Lisa's eyes, and she almost broke from hyptrolysis because of the pain.

"Babe, listen carefully. The Director rejected it. He said he'd put us at nine. But you and the kids need to scramble like we're at ten. This is for real. It's not a drill. Got it?"

"Will I ever see you again?"

"Babe, listen. If *you* act like we're at ten, you'll see me soon enough. But you and the kids need to go to ten. I don't have time to call them."

"I love you, Rex."

"Love you, babe."

J-rex hung up, frowning. His son was 17. It wouldn't be easy to convince Derrack to go to level ten without warning, and especially without hyptrolysis.

He was dialing Derrack when another alarm sounded, notifying him that the Decontamination Chamber was being entered. He smiled on hearing the alarm, glad that something still worked in all the wreckage. But he was also a little surprised the SecurPatrol had gotten back so quickly. Then he saw on the monitor that it was only a single figure entering the chamber. Lat.

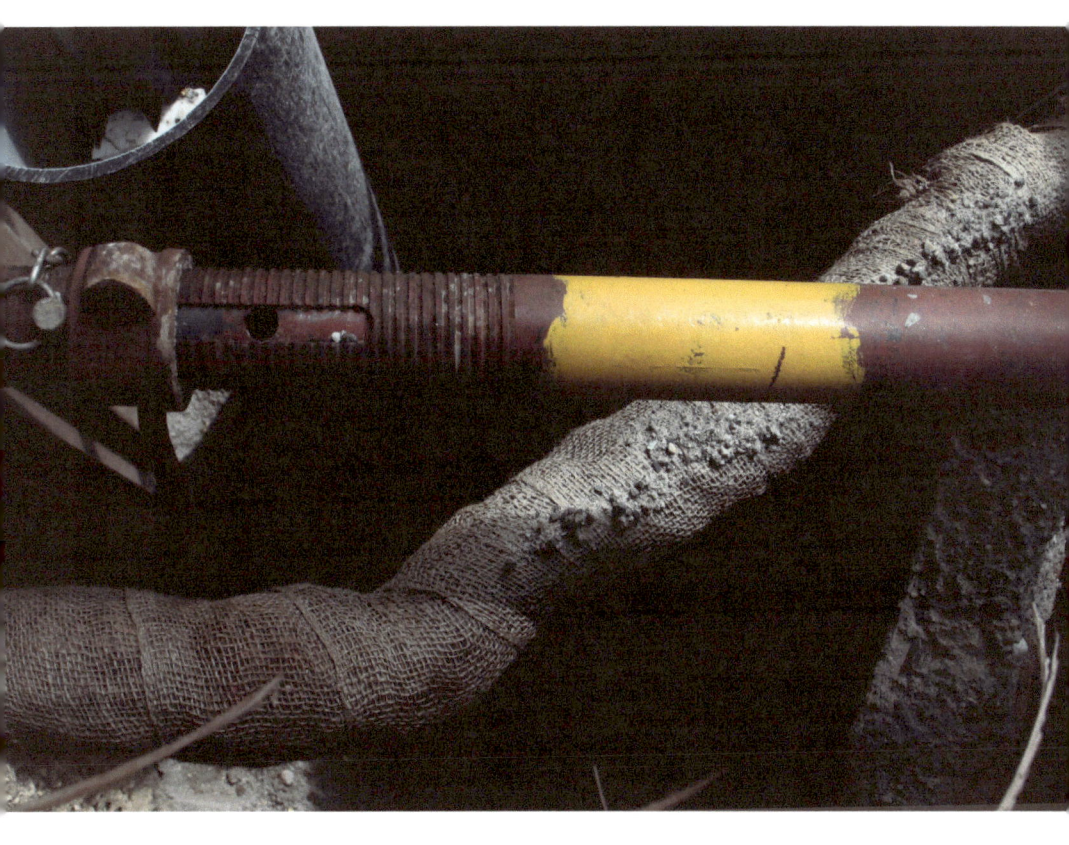

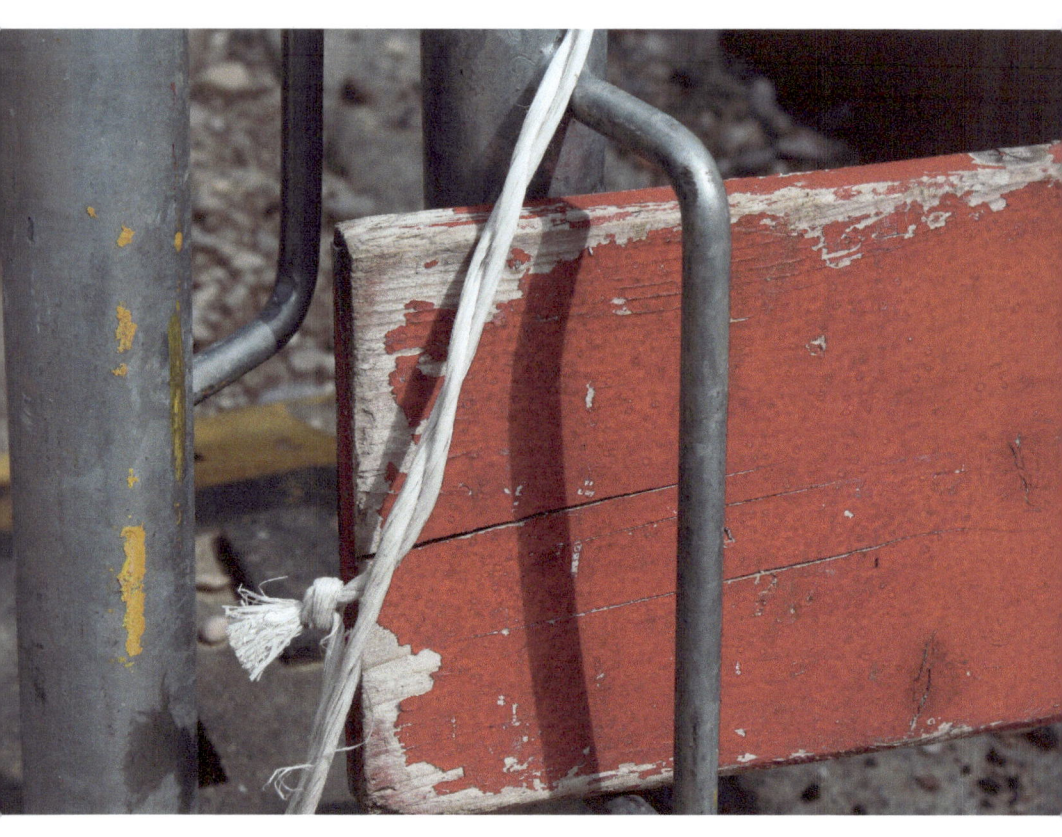

J-rex switched on the InfoCom. "Lat. Stay back. We need the SecurPatrol to go in first."

Lat didn't respond. He just kept moving forward, like he hadn't heard. J-rex repeated the command, and again got no response.

And then, for the first time, J-rex identified a part of the damage that he hadn't expected. The InfoCom was down. Lat couldn't hear him.

J-rex stiffened. J-rex had talked to the Director and Lisa on their phones. But he'd used InstaText to recall his team, and InstaText and the plant's InfoCom used the same channel.

As J-rex watched Lat heading towards the disaster, he realized that none of his earlier texts had gone out. The SecurPatrol hadn't gotten his text to provide backup. His team hadn't gotten his text to return. Except for Lat, none of his team had even turned around yet. They were all unaware of the recall, most of them still traveling *away* from the site. So far he hadn't actually told anyone about disaster except Lisa and the Director. . . .

But in a minute, one more person was going to know. Lat was in the Decontamination Chamber and was half way through the process. In less than sixty seconds, Lat would be in the thick of the smoke and the fire.

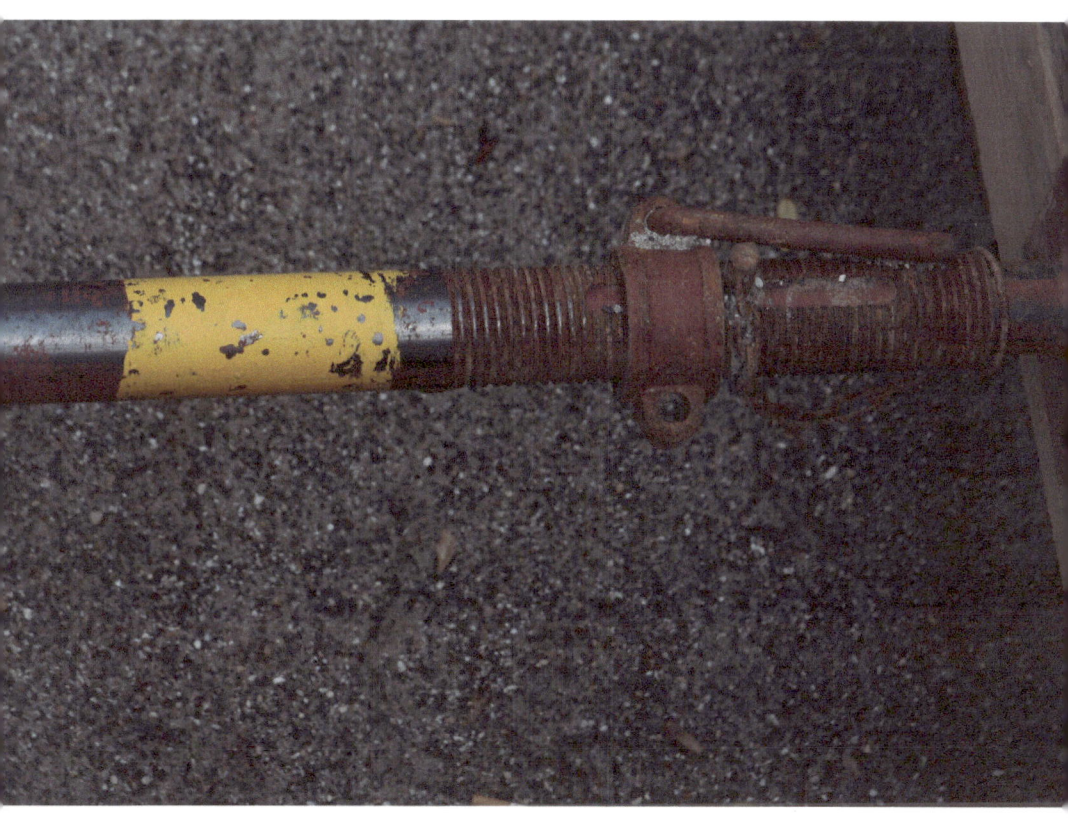

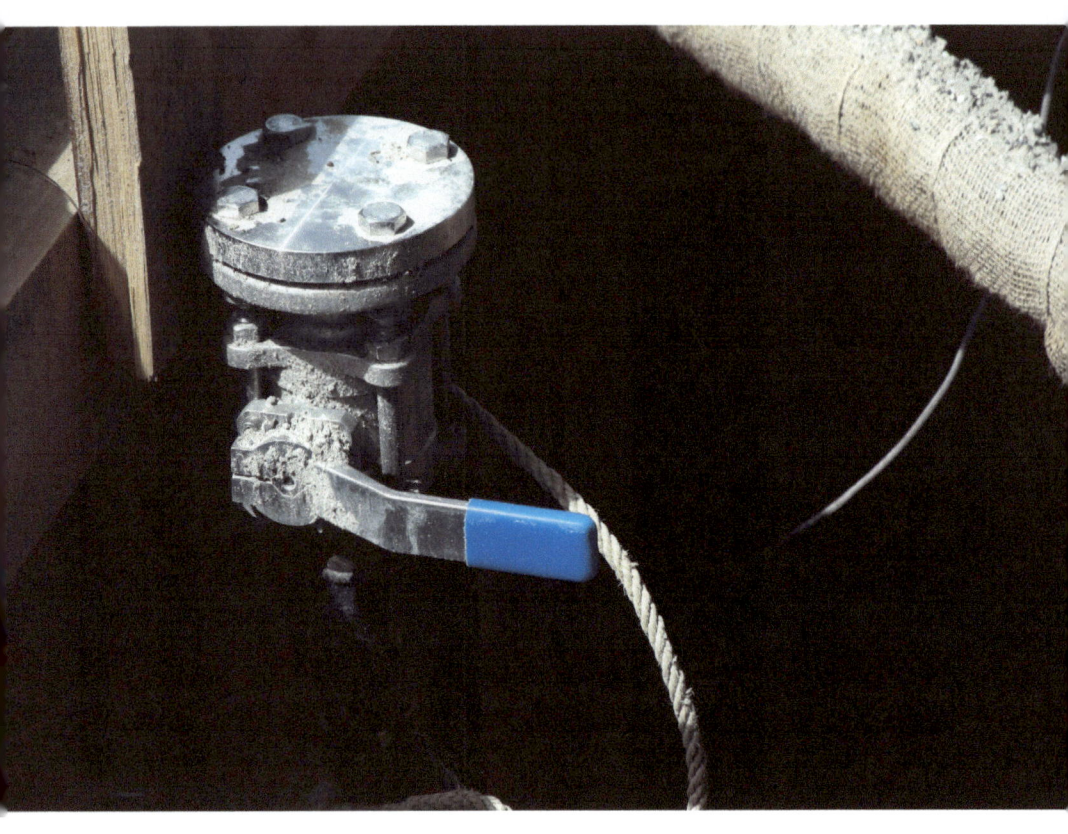

J-rex grabbed the phone to call Lat, then cursed, realizing that Lat would have followed protocol and left his phone outside the Decontamination Chamber. J-rex tried the back-up channels for the InfoCom but still couldn't get through. As he watched, the lights in the Decontamination Chamber indicated the sequence was complete. In five seconds the doors would open.

Lat was motionless, patiently waiting. And then he suddenly moved, hitting the emergency override and listening intently.

The doors to the chamber were so thick J-rex doubted any sound could have gotten through from the next room. But something had caught Lat's attention.

J-rex grabbed his phone and scrambled a call to Alice at the Plant Nine reception desk. She had access to a Corporate InfoCom system that was on a separate channel from the one the plant used. J-rex had her send out the InstaTexts he had tried to send earlier, wincing as he thought of the delay.

"Anything else, sir?" asked Alice. "I couldn't help notice that we've jumped to level seven."

"Seven?" J-rex said.

"We were at four just a few minutes ago – then five, now seven."

J-rex glanced at his own CorpChannel NewsFeed and noticed she was right. He tried to keep his tone neutral. "Thanks, Alice. If I need anything else, I'll call back. But do me a favor – call and let me know if the level changes any more today."

"Will do, sir. Out."

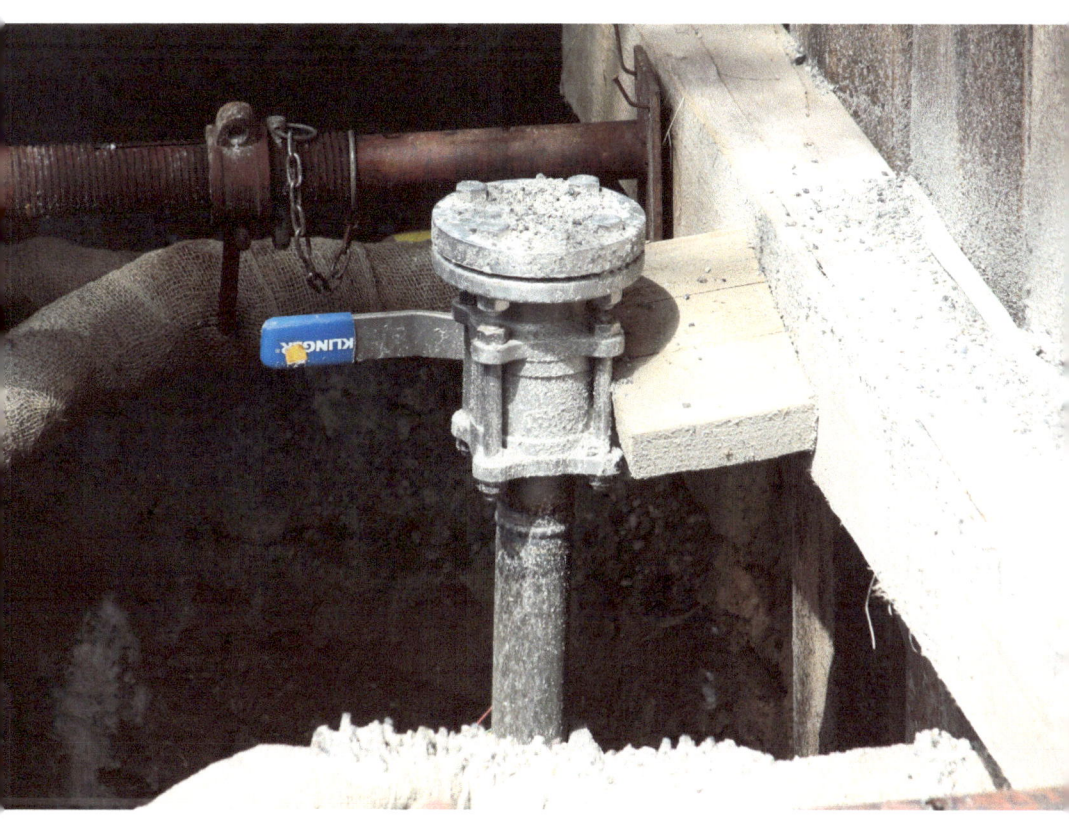

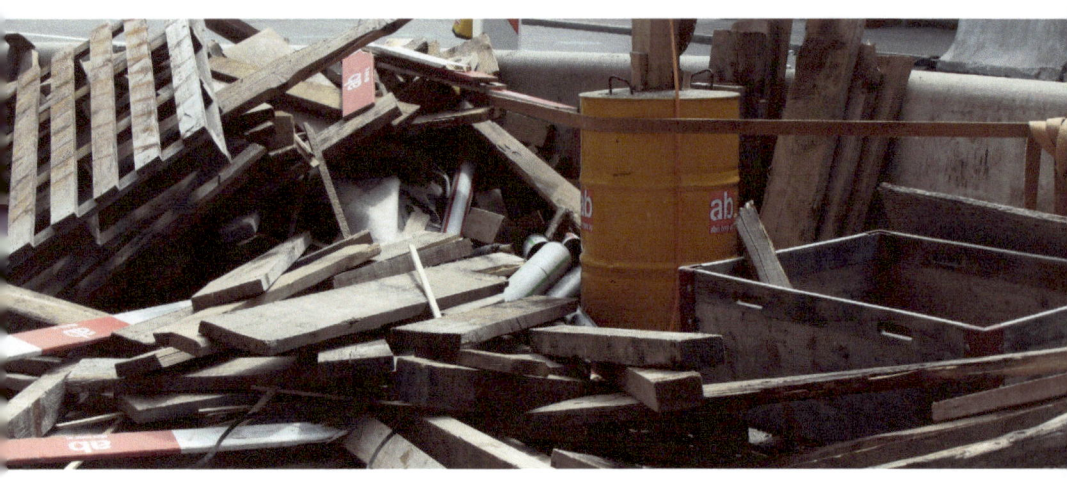

J-rex was furious. They had what was probably an all-out ten, a reason to destroy everything in the building, and the Director was cautiously increasing the levels as if they had time. Seven! If the SecurPatrol team arrived expecting level seven, they would be in for a rude shock.

J-rex guessed the Director was trying to get the Senators out of town before raising the levels further – but keeping the level suppressed wouldn't help his team to return with the haste he needed.

Lat had been staring at the doors of the Decontamination Chamber for a long time – then he shifted his gaze to the frame around it, then the wall. Inch by inch, he inspected the whole chamber.

J-rex realized Lat still didn't know what was wrong – he was just trying to follow up on his intuition that *something* was wrong.

Lat would probably ask permission to inspect the Decontamination Chamber with a scanner next, but first he was following protocol that no metal enter the chamber.

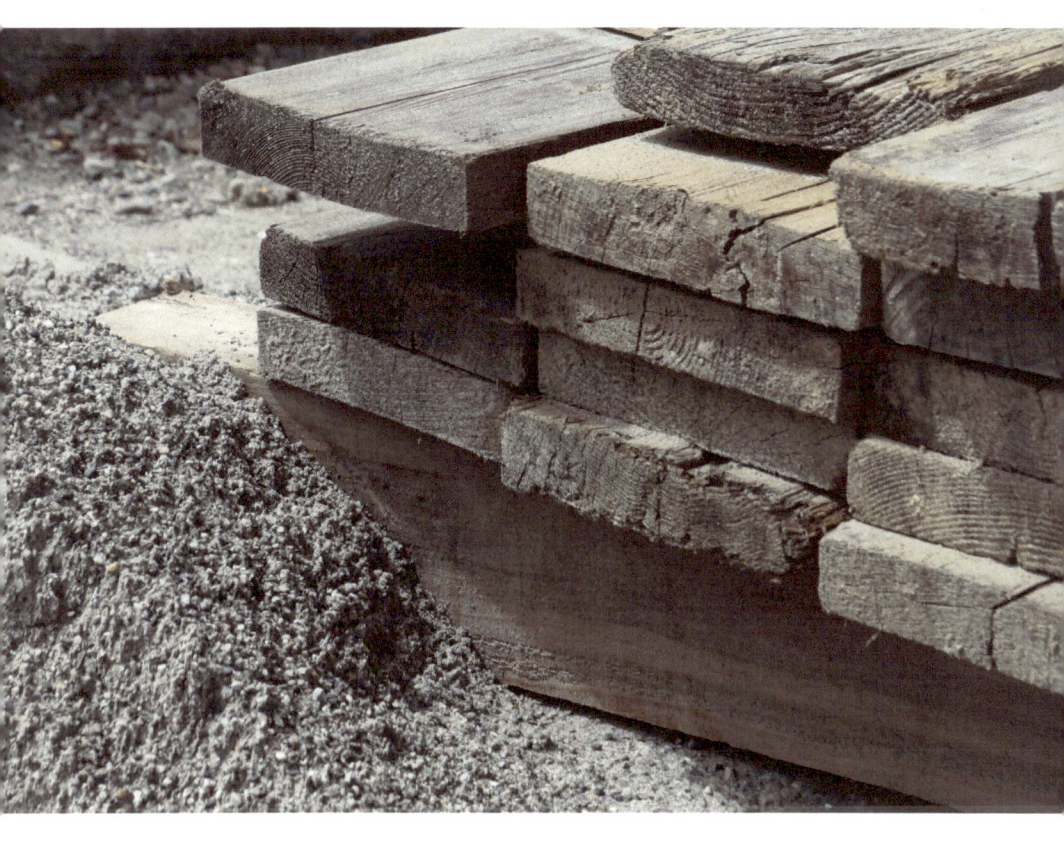

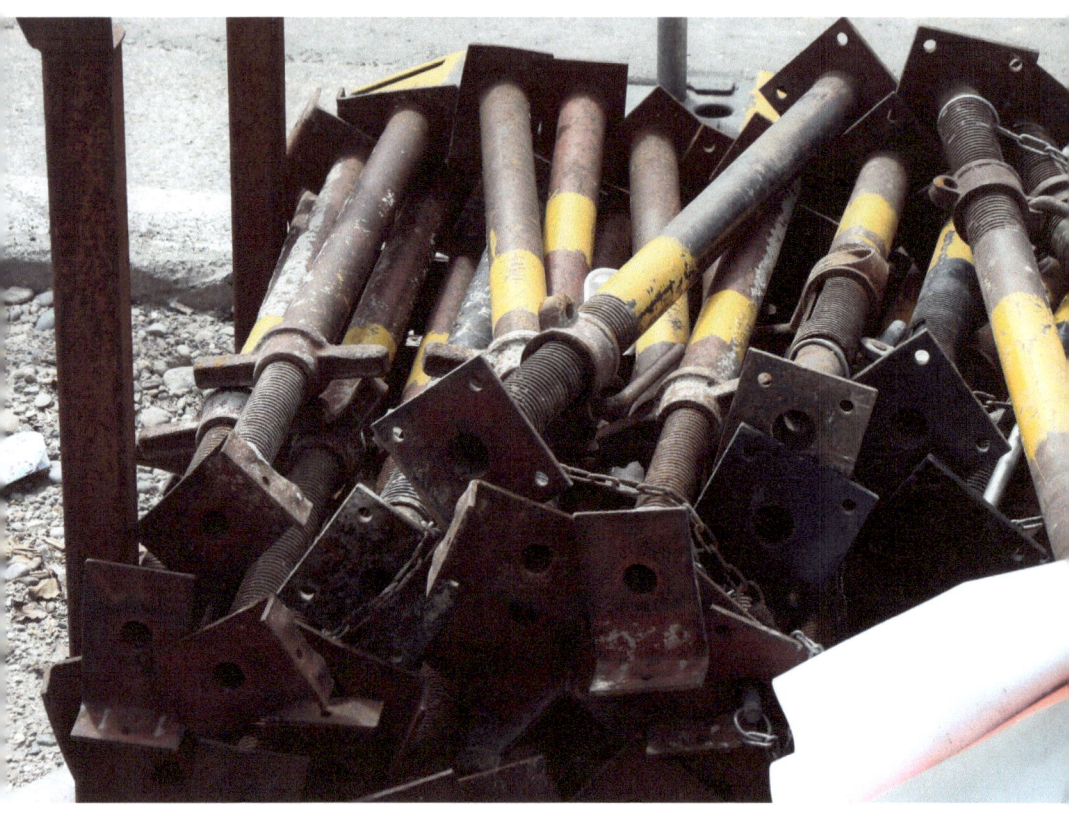

J-rex realized too late what Lat's next move would be. Lat hadn't hit the kill switch because he'd heard something. He'd hit the kill switch just to inspect the chamber more thoroughly. But now he was done with his inspection. He hadn't heard any of the mayhem in the next room. And he had no idea what waited for him on the other side of the doors. Lat reached over and released the emergency override. The clock reset to a ten-second countdown.

J-rex frantically tried one more time to get through on the InfoCom, but he could tell from Lat's blank expression that Lat couldn't hear. As J-rex watched, the countdown ended and the first doors slid open, then the second.

As the second doors opened, Lat was exposed to the whole scene: equipment smashed everywhere, fires, electric sparks, smoke, – and then the terrifying sound of a furious slithering as an alligator rushed straight towards Lat as fast as it could move.

~~

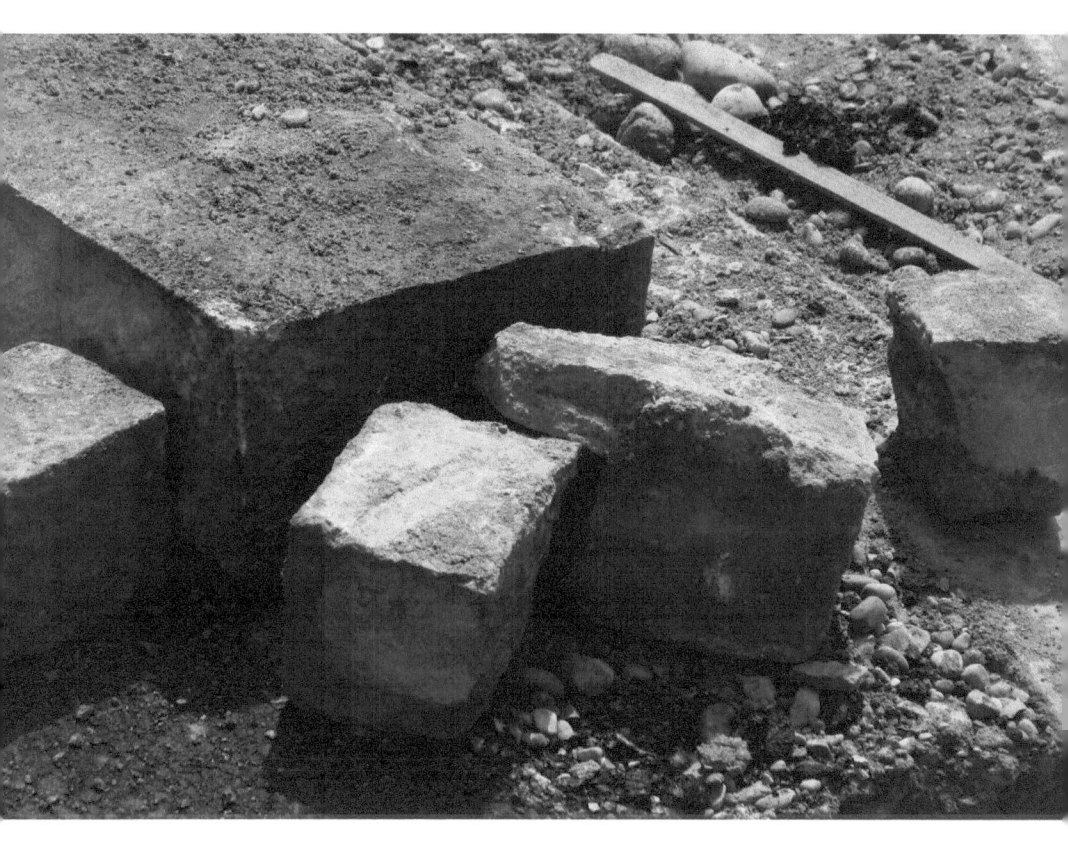

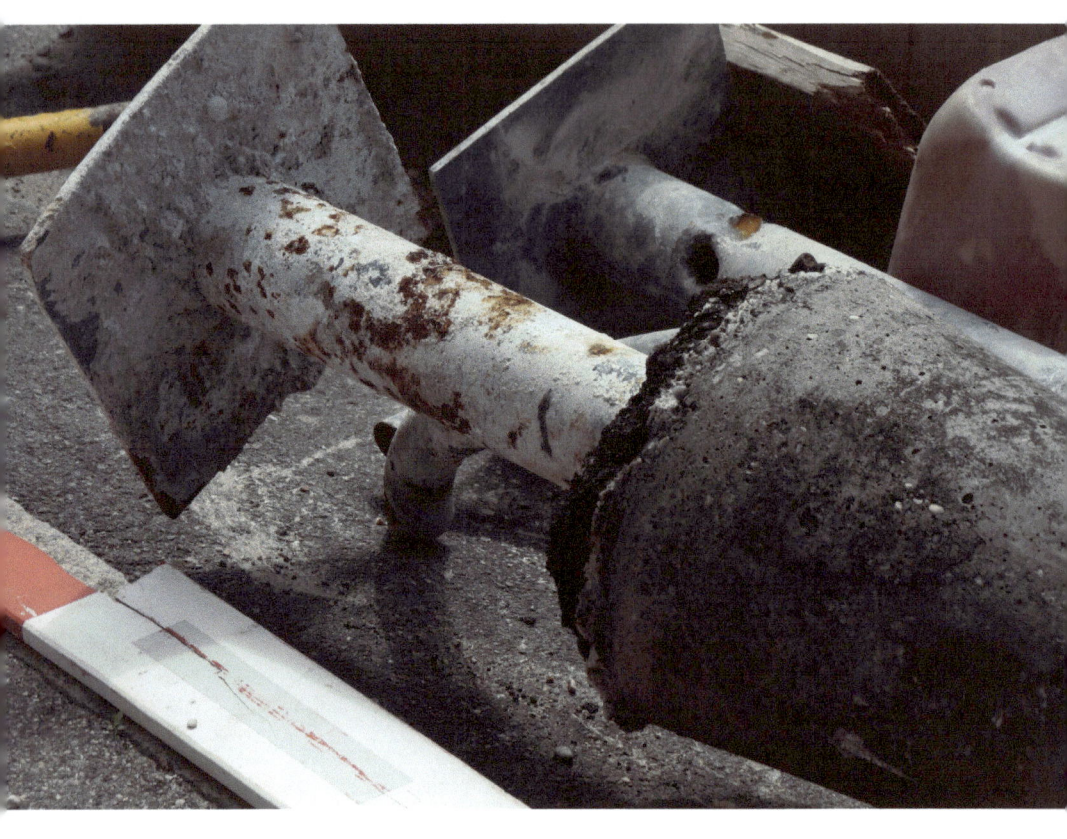

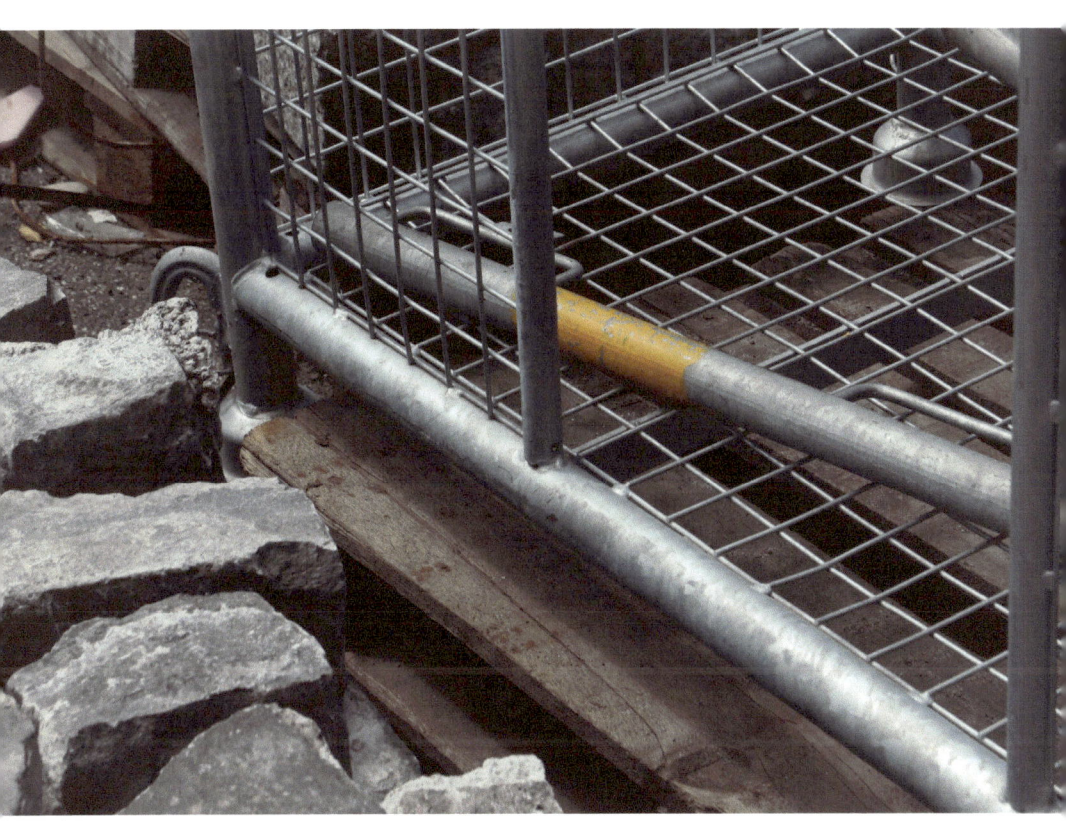

A Mark Dahle Portfolio

Lat's Collapse

Present Divestment #4

This Mark Dahle Portfolio includes a colorful abstract painting, twenty-five beautiful photographs from Basel, Switzerland, and a story about some problems with time travel.

Fifteen minutes before, the room had been sterile and clean. Now there was broken glass everywhere, smashed equipment, small fires, electric sparks showering from slashed wires, smoke, and, he finally saw, movement – a gator racing the length of the room straight towards Lat, moving as fast as it could go.

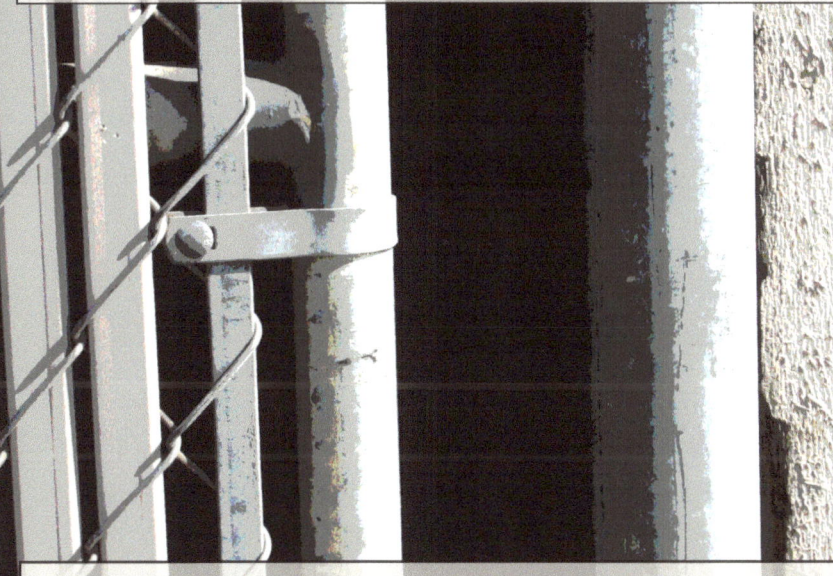

A Mark Dahle Portfolio

Derrack's Folly

Present Divestment #5

This Mark Dahle Portfolio includes a colorful abstract painting, twenty-six slightly altered photographs, and a story about a mom trying to stay calm in an emergency.

Lisa smiled and relaxed. In five minutes she'd be at the school picking up her kids. This was going to be easy.

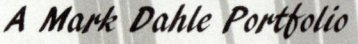

A Mark Dahle Portfolio

Escape

Present Divestment #6

This Mark Dahle Portfolio includes a colorful abstract painting, twenty-five gorgeous photographs from Florida, and a story about a family trying to escape disaster.

Lisa pulled down her jacket and walked briskly into the entrance to the employment office. Earlier she had thought it would be easy to pick up her kids. Now she wondered if she had any chance at all to get her son. She had too much experience already with the Feast.